Turn Left at Normal

by Laura Rodley

Turn Left at Normal © 2018 Laura Rodley. All rights reserved. Big Table Publishing Company retains the right to reprint. Permission to reprint must be obtained from the author, who owns the copyright.

ISBN: 978-1-945917-23-3

Printed in the United States of America

Front Cover Photo: James Rodley
Back Cover Photo: Lily Thompson
Author Photo: Lily Thompson

Also by Laura Rodley:

Rappelling Blue Light
Your Left Front Wheel is Coming Loose
As You Write It, A Franklin County Anthology, Volumes 1-VI
Counter Point

"Making other books jealous since 2004"

Big Table Publishing Company
Boston, MA
www.bigtablepublishing.com

Table of Contents

Ettalynn	9
Resurrection	10
Thirty Canada Geese	13
Double Take	14
Interior Decorating	15
Drying Grass	16
Rehobeth	18
Rebel	19
Halibut Run	20
Bounty	22
Tuesday's Storm	23
Mowing	24
Breakwater	25
Catapult	26
Not Yet	27
Initiate	28
Given	30
Crush	31
Sunrise	32
Night-walking	33
Farmer's Yoga	34
County Fair	36
Down South	37
Seaside	38
Right Whales at Race's Point	40
Drops of Mercy	42
Birds of Mercy	44
Mud Daubers	47
Fresh from the Vine	48
The Language of Animals	50
Wings	52

In the Clouds	53
Sluice	54
The Divinity of Chocolate	56
Coda	58
Clemency	59
The Treasures of the Earth	60
Released Back into the Wind	62
Angle	64
The Other Ninety-eight Percent	66
Knowing the Great Unknown	67
Invincible	68
Basic Training	69
Early Thanksgiving Migration	70
Barren	71
Desert Sand	72
Right of First Refusal	73
Hospice Nurse Drives Home	74
Commissioned	76
Thanksgiving	77
California's Rose	78
Beards of Moss	79
Taking Off	80
The Distance	81
Land of the Living	82
Return of the Tigers	83
Saving the World	84
Cormorants	85
Blinded by the Sun	86
Moving Up the Coast	87
First Swim	88
Crossing the Great Divide	89

Acknowledgements

"Resurrection" – Pushcart Prize winner

"Thirty Canada Geese", "Mowing", "Catapult", "Angle" "The Other Ninety-eight Percent", "Early Thanksgiving Migration", Right of First Refusal", "Taking Off"," Land of the Living", "Moving Further Up the Coast" – *New Verse News*

"Halibut Run" – Editor's Choice, *Unrorean*, and 2nd Place, Poets Seat Poetry Contest

"Tuesday's Storm" and "Double Take" – *Unrorean*

"Coda" – nominated for a Pushcart Prize

"Given", "Night-walking", "Rehobeth", "Down South" (in interview), "Wings", "Commissioned", "Beards of Moss", and "Saving the World" – *Boston Literary Magazine*

"Initiate" and "Fresh from the Vine" – *Solace in So Many Words*

"Basic Training", "Rebel", "Drops of Mercy", "The Treasures of the Earth", "The Divinity of Chocolate" – *Naugatuck River Review*

"Seaside" – *Sahara, Rappelling Blue Light*

"Birds of Mercy" – *Earth's Daughters, Your Left Front Wheel is Coming Loose*

"The Language of Animals" and "Released Back into the Wind" – *What's Nature got to Do with Me? Staying Wildly Sane in a Mad World* by Native West Press

"Crush" and "Sluice" – *Silkworm*

"Sunrise" – *Stone Walls II*

"California's Rose" – *Aurorean*

"Blinded by the Sun" – *Penwood Review*

"The Distance" and "Return of the Tigers" – *Montague Reporter*

For Jim Rodley

Ettalynn

Arise young child
and come to view the sea;
three weeks old you are and it is time.
Stand in my arms as we hold the sun
in our arms, like we hold you,
as you were held in your mother's arms,
invisible, inside the sea waters in her belly
where you grew, speck of dust and dreams,
where you grew, to the tide of her ocean
up and down as she walked. Invisible
you held your staff of light, your heart,
and sluiced out of the sea
when her tide ran out
and you came in, raising
your voice in quiet exaltation,
barely a whimper as you were
laid in her arms, outside
in the air where you must now
breathe, young mermaid
until your father cut
the cord and you left
your silkie's armor behind.

Resurrection

Never again will a tsunami
come silently out of the unknown,
it will be tracked by radar
so there will be just enough
time to run.
Never again
will people walk unaided
by the spirits of those
drowned by the tsunami;
smell this rose for me
they will say, dipping
their head closer as
if for a kiss,
taste this smoked eel
for me as they lean
by your cheek
to hear you chew,
touch this they will say
willing you to lean towards
the magnolia bud
ripe with the wish to burst
but not yet the pink halo erupts.
Carry this, they ask
carry this load of bamboo
tied with rope upon my back
take this load to my mother
tell her I got lost upon the way
and now in deep waters of the ocean
I have not forgotten.

Untie the bundle for her,
her hands knotted with age,
lay the bamboo in a neat pile
for her to use as she wishes.
She had so admired the way
I cut the stalks without
bruising their ends;
it takes a clean, sharp knife.
Tell her I am calling her name,

speak it for me,
Mamasan, my little Rebecca,
speak it for me
so she can dry her tears.
And for my brother,
pull his hands away
from the damp soil,
tell him I am not here,
he will never find my bones,
but you have found me,
oh kind stranger,
walking beside you
and you will tell him
what I say; I beg you,
and I am not ashamed of that.

And take these slippers
for my sister, red with
embroidered flowers, beaded.
They were for her birthday,
tell her I have not forgotten
I was just looking for a way
back in to bring them to her,
a way back in.

Tell them, forgive me
for not having followed
the flight of the birds
who flew inland two days before
away from the ocean,
the gulls, the bitterns, the terns;
they knew what was coming
but I turned my head.

Thirty Canada Geese

You do not know it
oh people of Japan
but thirty Canada geese
are holding the ground in place
here on the other side
of the world, in a field
laying fallow, their feet prickled
by the sheared-off cornstalks.
They nestle on the dark mud
in places where you would
search for your houses,
your friends, your families, their bodies.
These geese chose this mud
here to hold the earth
in place just for you,
so you can remember
how to rebuild it,
their tucking their heads
under their wings
a constant prayer.

Double Take

If you are alive, then so must I be
Your skin pale beige, a tourniquet of hope, perfectly free
For the price of a kiss, the green edge of ash leaves
Flouncing on window glass, guarding us from the sun that grieves

Your skin pale beige, a tourniquet of hope, perfectly free
The green sea of your eyes, the graying curls, fingerprints worn
Flouncing on window glass, guarding us from the sun that grieves
So dark behind its back, it cannot see the world's reaching plaid sleeves

Your skin pale beige, a tourniquet of hope, perfectly free
Wake me if you need me, you say, holding my head securely
The green sea of your eyes, the graying curls, fingerprints worn
From grasping steering wheels, full buckets, picking corn

Flouncing on window glass, guarding us from the sun that grieves
For the price of a kiss, the green edge of ash leaves
Behind its back, so dark it cannot see the world's reaching plaid sleeves
If you are alive, then so must I be.

Interior Decorating
After Yusef Komunyakaa

As if our minds were double-jointed,
we bent over backwards and then backwards
again, a human pretzel that the circus
rejected. They had dozens of them
and they always tipped over, right, left,
sideways; instead of one attraction,
the attraction needed a spotter.
So we took our minds to the bleachers
and stepped up the trunks of elephants
who gently placed us on their backs
and we pulled the feet out of the crook
of our minds, one foot by one foot,
then we wrangled the hands,
the pelvic bone, the ribs, curled
like potato chips and we rocked
with the rollicking sway that elephants
have when on their way
to the watering hole and there they submerged,
splashed water with the force of a fire-hose,
spraying us towards shore
and there we crawled, spun like isinglass,
and learned to walk again without falling.

Drying Grass

Mama, you never showed me how to drive a car, use only one foot
for gas and brake.
You never showed me where the brake was, you pulled it off, left
the brake space open;
I crawled through it, I was so little. But now I'm tall, and Mama,
I can't sew the brake

pedal back on. I push it to the sky, and the sky won't take it back.
I press the brake to my heart,
like a pillow, and I can't keep my heart in, it swallows me as though
it is a large quilt
and I am the seeds inside an orange. You never told me
what love was like,

you only left a hole where love poured in. I could not stand at the dam
like the little Dutch Boy,
keep the dam from breaking, I grew tired of standing there,
I took my finger out. And see,
Mama, all the love came rushing in; the emus' black eyes, the llamas'

peculiar upper lips, the stiff hairs on the haflingers Mitchell, and
Madison's muzzles, the sharp kick
the cows give the empty water trough, the spray of the water
filling it, the red handle
of the pump that must stay erect to fill it, keep the lines open. The
pitchfork

prongs, hay I toss down to the sheep, the muruph bleat the sheep
makes that got pushed aside,
didn't grab hers, the second trip up the stairs, the wooden slats
of the heavy trap door on the floor
I heave open, my shoulders as I thrust more large clumps, the dust,

the trap hole I almost fall through, the trap door as I lift it, drop it
closed, the water spigot
I turn off, bathtub full now, the cria's long eyelashes, her tiny nose
as she sniffs me.
She's less than a day old and knows me; when she was inside it,
I pushed against her

Mama's belly and she kicked against my hands. The scraping
of the shovel as I muck out
manure startles her. Mama, there's swallows nesting on the roof,
a luna moth by my doorway,
velvet on my sewing machine, soft feathers lining the breast
of the white

chicken my daughter Emma pats in her arms. There's tall seeded grass,
June's first cutting, a grouse
and her tiny chick, she doesn't scatter, she's heard our car many times,
there's tiny nests
hidden in these fields, eggshells broken open, hard wood fence posts
resist nails

pounded into them, barbed wire sharp and heavy, black flies dense.

Rehobeth

I hold onto the slightly oily
shoulders of my father as he swims
way out at Rehobeth beach, leaving

the beach revelers way behind
going out, out, out past the sandbar
going far above both our heads.

Certainly I cannot swim back in or let go.
I am five years old, or less, so I watch
as we pass everyone who is out in the water

as we keep going. Back on the beach
lifeguards call people back out of the water,
and they emerge, dripping salt brine

off their suits but my father keeps going
and my head gets very hot. When
we return they have caught the shark

that had been lurking in the water
and hung him up for all to see.

Rebel

In Mattinicus Marta wore no shirt
as she hauled up the lobster traps,
pulled the clicking

bodies out of the traps, set the
salty herring through the circular net
in the new bait bag

and dropped it down again, first pulling
the buoy rope tight, clicking the hook
that holds the trap so it

wouldn't be swallowed by the sea or
moved by the current
and then she steered the boat around

another shoal, inhaling
her cigarette deeply with one hand
as the other hand held the wheel by the motor,

dreaming of the big house
she and Ambrose would buy, and how many
more traps she had to pull up before the

day was over, noon. Work almost done,
too soon she had to pull her shirt back
over her chest, too soon she had to cover

herself up like a woman again
when she had wished so hard
that she had been born a boy.

Halibut Run

Marcus turns the wheel a fraction,
squints more than usual to see
through the snow-thick fog, fog horn
deceptive in its echoes; ten
or 100 feet ahead could be the dock.
The sea has swallowed the markers.
He's swimming in the fog's dampness,
luckily lighter than the black water
he rides on, only a film below, even so.
How will he find the edge of his nets,
the batteries for the lights blown from the damp.
How, by counting, compass
and caution, to wait it out means
drifting off course, to turn back
means a day's lost wages, and it
will lift he promises himself, it will.

He knocks three metal buckets
against the gunwale, their clanging
reminds him of gunshots in the weighing shed,
territory wars, one shot dead
center yet he lives, his heart
spits out the bullet, lodges in
the pericardium, doctors amazed he
survives; just one more miracle.
Marcus sees them every day.
His wife sees one every time
he walks in the door, his slicker
and boots hung in the outside shed,
attempting to keep the smell of fish
out of the house, but it's in his fingers

as he pulls her to him, it's in his kiss
as he calms her fears, assures her
he's really there, he's safe, as his tongue
becomes the leg of a clam digging
on the beach of her mouth, as
smooth as the inside of an abalone shell.

Bounty

Winching up three tons of cod, halibut,
Marcus dumps the bounty on the deck.
One fish wears a brown suit;

a man's body siphoned from the
ocean's sleep. His face more mollusk
than a man's, his hands more

seaweed than hands, a ring still
attached, inscribed Martin and Marky
12/2/79. How did he get here,

over-dressed for the job as lobsterman.
Inside the pockets of pants, Marcus gingerly
searches for and pulls out a sodden wallet, pockmarked

by salt, inside pictures of a blonde
haired woman, two smiling toddlers
and what might have been him, a wide smiling

man blonde hair toasted by the sun, his arms
stretched round woman and children, content.

Tuesday's Storm

She dared me, she says, dripping sea water and rain
half the size of the darer, who claims, *We're being brave,*
ocean grey and furious, smashing froth at their feet, a slave
ready to reel them in as they flee back up sand dunes, taunting.

Half the size of the darer, who claims, *We're being brave.*
Or mermaids, I suggest, wondering, where is your mother,
ready to reel them in as they flee back up sand dunes, taunting.
I continue walking to the crest, return, no girls, just their haunting.

Half the size of the darer, who claims, *We're being brave.*
A bittern mewls, their footsteps lead away: no watery grave.
Or mermaids, I suggest, wondering, where is your mother,
no one else cresting shoreline, waves crashing, foaming white braids.

Ready to reel them in as they flee back up sand dunes, taunting
ocean grey and furious, smashing froth at their feet, a slave.
I continue walking to the crest, return, no girls, just their haunting.
She dared me, she says, dripping sea water and rain.

Mowing

Over the railroad tracks
the fields were full of baby rabbits
and when the mower came,
it strew the litter of their nests
like motorists threw cans out their windows.
I picked up two baby rabbits,
small as tablespoons with ears,
soft as the purple beards of an iris,
crossed the railroad tracks,
and walked back home.
No, you cannot keep them
so back across the tracks
I had orders not to cross
and down into the newly mowed grass
I placed them, covered them
with clover blossoms,
and hoped their mothers
would not smell the touch of me, a human,
upon their fur, a mixture of grey, black and white,
fluff of clouds here on earth.

Breakwater

Your father's thumbs stick out above his head
as you reach for them with your hands
and climb your feet through the water

up to his shoulders, his skin slightly oily.
You stand, wobbling as if first born,
let go his thumbs.

He grabs your ankles
as you press your hands together
as if in prayer.

He crouches and
one, two, three,
springs up as you dive

clear sailing into the water.
He doesn't catch you:

you are meant to fall,
he's let you go.

Catapult

Close to the forest duff
the jack-in-the-pulpits
held their sermons,
leaves striped and curled,
their fairy dome bud
beaming light
to passersby,
even the hobos
that lit their fires
far enough away
from the Windybush pool
that swimmers could not smell their smoke
and heated their cans of beans
and black bread
to sup in the wild
where maybe God
could hear their prayers,
and that of the squirrel
and deer who wanted
an end to hunting season.
One hobo left his sole-
worn boot, threads ripped,
sole curled under from the damp
just like the curled pulpit leaf,
both claimed by the intensity
of their constant prayer, ceaseless search.

Not Yet

Twilight drops its cape upon the farmer's hands,
the mallet he pounds against the post
rearing before him as a dimwit ghost

too hungry for comfort to stay away
the ghost follows his hand as the post sways

deeper into the ground, so dimly lit.
The pounder wishes he could be done, quit

but five more posts in the break in the fence
must be installed, against the mare's defense

lest she wander into neighbor's close field
and nibble their grain, a harvest yield.

So long past his staying power the man
aims ghostly mallet towards four-inch wing span
of the resisting post edge, takes his stand.

Initiate

It was George who taught me how to harness
the willing halflingers but must confess
it was they who taught me to have patience
standing quietly, lifting heads to inch

the pillowed collars over their long ears,
lean my face by their teeth, letting go fears
as they stood breathing in and out, no stress
as I threaded the black leads of harness

through rings and down their backs, clicked them out
of stalls, then hitched together, turn-about,
back up towards the shafts of cart, then feed
the shafts through the harness, buckle, the need

for perfection paramount, then lead out
these willing beauties, haw, gee, for sunny bout.
In the freezing January weather
the horses pulled the wagon, now tethered

together, bells on harness ringing, wide
hooves slipping on ice patches, cannot hide
what surprises January decides,
you must endure, down the track, stopping slides

in training, round the barn, then at a lope
back again round the barn and up the slope
horses pulling on the bit eagerly
passing the sheep, emus, border collie

Holly trotting by their side, dodging dirt
 and ice kicked up by their hooves, always flirt
-ing with danger, just as we all were, learn
-ing something new, lessening call to yearn.

Given

I was given these two hands,
these two feet; I was given them
without asking and they are mine.
With my feet on your body I do walk
on frozen ground where coyotes step,
fishers, raccoons, and quail.
With my breath I inhale
your sweet liquor, the cold snap
of four degrees; how my lungs
crave your air inside me,
its green perfume, though now
your body is slick with ice,
hard with frost, tasting green
though I must cover my mouth
with a purple scarf to take you in.
Each morning this is how I wake,
with you upon my lips.

Crush

Inside the second story
of the sawmill shed,
I pull away the full shovel
from the heap.
The layered lines of the sawdust
are wet, red, beige, dusk and tan.
I slide it to the door, heave it
towards the waiting mouth of the tractor,
silver shovelful after shovelful,
bedding for the horses and cows.
He waits, tractor turned off,
sitting solid on the worn black seat.
I know he's down there,
wondering what it would be like,
if the lines of the coursing down sawdust
are cool like my skin,
its color, the blush of my cheeks.
The loader is full, he lowers its mouth,
chugs the tractor away.
The last shovelful I throw towards it
drops like dry fluttering rain,
the sawdust room almost empty,
except for me.

Sunrise

She breaks the morning,
sighs as the rain parts birch leaves
smatters upon her roof.
She does not stay under cover,
wanders in the warmth of summer's rain
drenching her cinnamon coat,
how she needs no yellow raincoat
or umbrella, just my eyes
upon her to make this morning
perfect, reaching for new grass
amongst fresh burdock,
burrs that catch in her mane.
Cooling off, I stand beside her,
drenching rain loosening burrs
and a hair oil of her own making
rubbed between my fingers as I pull
them out, lean my forehead
against her warm neck.
She breaks the morning,
this sunrise I watch for
in colors of white and caramel,
reds and pinks already past.

Night-walking

The coyotes' close yipping enters
doorways I did not know I had,
slinging open windows shut tight
against the cold, the shiver of fear;
they're so close while I walk my dog
I must get home fast, shiver of maybe
I'll see one circling with my flashlight.
More yipping, then barking like a dog
to the left though no one right here owns one,
the same coyote that barked earlier this winter,
barking, impatient for me and Tyndall to go inside
so he could pad the road we walk on.
So quickly he passed, that even before
I could return outside,
he left a line of prints, a single file line
in the new snow.

Farmer's Yoga

Bending knees, hip and back
parallel to taut fence line
the narrow foot of space
he bends his body through
holding barbed wire above him,
steady, slow, no haste—
haste causes tears in clothing
or fingers—then the stretch
up to the highest bales,
the thump the fifty pounds
of green fragrant dried grass
makes against his bunched thighs,
the doctors warned him against this
lifting, but he stretches his two
arms long, holds the pose,
balancing two fifty pounders,
horses hungry, bumping his shoulder,
the long horse moves as he breaks
open the bales, splashing
the flakes onto dry ground
later the long stretch of his arm
a slow steady reach in a cow's privates
checking her calf during the long wait
of her labor, how his arm stretches longer
than seems possible as her contractions
clamp his biceps,
later he reaches again, searching
for what has fallen behind his seat
in the tractor, the stretched wings

of a heron, his fingers feathers
clasping the hat he was searching for,
a hat his father wore
of canvas, bent with a wire rim,
once round as the Os of the cow,
the rim bends anyway needed
just like his son's body
now wings settling
closed against his side,
hands steady upon the wheel.

County Fair

Tri-county fair, dim of summer, so hot
the rabbits need ice cubes behind ears, spot
checks of water, flowers on display wilt
without constant spray, excitement full tilt.
Will we get first prize, will Emma's pet win,
can't keep her patient, when judging begins.
She holds her rabbit high in her short arms
as long as she is tall, gently, no harm
comes to her from scratches, her rabbit's come
to trust her, wiggles his nose, smells cotton
candy, sugared apples, pie, forgotten
hamburgers, remembered French Fries, soda,
the Ferris wheel high in the sky, wave
to people, bun, gives him carrot she saved.

Down South

Down south dry pan soil, armadillos
wide-spread hats, shorts, pecans, Tiparillos

cousin's father smoked, combed his eyebrows
with a mustache comb, cattle ranches, not cows,

herds spread on land so far it takes a plane
to span what's owned, what's not taken by man,

here and there houses their father had built,
architect by trade, solid ground, no silt

like my father's job, an engineer, dream
to become a teacher, left it all, top cream

as he was, king of the hill but kings want
more than they see or know, take a jaunt

into other territories uncharted
all they need, endless funds to get started.

Seaside

Maybe it's the peanut butter and jelly sandwiches
clotted with sand or the beach blanket
you try so carefully not to shake its sand across

your neighbor but the wind picks it up,
flaps its collection upon the lotioned back
of the man sleeping with his head under a newspaper,

the hairs on his back bleached white, his skin red,
maybe it's how you want it to be perfect but it seldom is,
it is just this wish to swim buoyant in salt water

where your body has no impact,
you are salt water joined inside salt water,
wild with the waves, you must protect

your skin from burning just like anybody else.
Maybe it's the treacherousness
of waves, how you were pulled

out towards the black rocks of the jetty,
the short choppy waves at Ocean Grove
hiding the tremendous undertow.

When your brother, home from college,
swam to get you, a dark wave crashed you
on his head; he turned back,

your father yelling something you cannot hear,
the boats in the distance not so far away.
Arms flailing like a zodiac wheel, unable to see,

you fight your way back through gray green foam,
bathing suit filled with crushed shells, stones
as you hit bottom, stagger out,

your father's so glad to see you. Maybe it's because
you share this love with him, something bigger than yourself,
this endless reaching, and it never says no.

Maybe because you both love this wild beast
lining the whole coast it's easier to love each other
or remember when you did.

Right Whales at Race's Point

They could be two centuries old,
the same time line as bow whales.
Can you imagine?
Swimming before submarines submerged,
before speedboats,
before nuclear weapons,
but not before whaling boats
used their brother's oil to light their way.
How silent the water must have been,
except for the song of the whales
crooning to each other,
dolphins clicking their sonar,
before airplanes
before barges of waste
were dumped in their playground,
before you and I were born.
And there they swim, underwater
45 minutes holding their breath
caressed by the smooth muscle
of the water, its cool hand
cooling them down, with no idea,
or even the thought of, extinction,
just the water warms up
and it's harder to find their friends.
But now off Race's Point coastal watchdogs
have stopped the boats from churning
or dropping their nets where whales feed,
gorging themselves on plankton
tiny pink dots that fill their
cavernous bellies, plankton
that they gave up for Lent

on their sojourn off Georgia's coast,
having rolled waves away on their journey
instead of a rock to rise again as Christ did
to break free at Easter
and sup once again.
On shore, I reach down, dip my hands
into the grey green tongues of waves
that have licked the backs
of these right whales
swimming off shore
only 100 yards away.
I do not dry my hands.

Drops of Mercy

Speak to me of changelings,
yellow leaves, spun of erupted buds
given to the children who reach their hands
scrambling out of piles of the dead at Auschwitz
searching for their parents,
give them these finely veined orange
layers of the tree's skin to sew
their eyes back on, so they can see
the leaves now for themselves.
Reach back, pull them out of the pit,
give them clogs with no splinters,
give them back the dress torn off;
one such good little girl out of so many,
obeying instructions did not pan out.
But now, follow the leader
of the leaves, let them drift
studded with sunlight-
a second birth- as they drift to the ground
where the little girl from Auschwitz
steps first into the clogs, then the threadbare dress,
opens her eyes, holds her hand out
for this fresh delight, all the leaves
covering the ground before she remembers.
Bring her hands forward,
fill them with yellow beech
crimson maple, purple aster, plum leaves
of hydrangea, pull her to you
be the mother she cannot find
be the father she left behind
be the sister whose name she cannot speak

she was too young to say it correctly
fill her arms with leaves,
kneel down so she can meet your eyes
be the one she's calling for,
fill the void, carry her home
don't let her go.

Birds of Mercy

Ah, the sparrows fluttering
the oracles of my heart
beat the tom-tom of the hereafter
beat the tom-tom of seed, sunflower, nutmeg
crack the omen of autumn
its pumpkin scented promise
how its arms are not too small
to wrap around us all.
Filbert shaped ventricles,
even filbert-sized, thump in
the breast of the nuthatch, cresting
the porch railing for more corn
more barley, how can I deny
him, he makes such an effort
zooming through rain, snow and sleet
a mailman delivering silent
promises, the I do, I will,
I eat, I live, I do not
succumb to the mantle of winter.

Inside my sister's heart
does there beat a small winsome sparrow
the tiny bird pumping its two inch long wings
against her ribs, does the sparrow
long to fly aboard her tongue and sing?
And what would he sing?
The red and golds of autumn leaves,
the blues and greens of delphinium and leaf
the browns and blues of heartache
with no relief.

Should I give her a plateful
of sparrows for her to swallow
folded up in tablet size
so inside her they flap
all her sorrow closer to the air,
up her throat, into her mouth
so she can sing, sing, and never
have to keep her mouth closed?

Here my sister, a plate of tablet sized sparrows
a canopy of thrushes for you to wear as a cape
the muted colors of brown and beige and cream you wear
and here the freckles on your face
are the speckles on the wood thrushes' breast,
around your feet the pecking peace of bantams.
Blue necked with emerald sheen
in front of you on branches in the oak tree
in your yard so you can see them from your 3rd floor apartment
eight mourning doves coo their gentle love song
singing your song, just for you over and over again.

The mourning doves pull tiny wagons in the trees,
their nests that they filled with eggs
three times this speckled summer so full of mist and rain.
Into the air fly the fledglings, the size of my fist
braving thunderstorms, creaking of branches,
the frantic bills of barred owls,
to scoot through the humid air, their heart,
their heart that they are always wearing
on their wings, wearing their heart
so that you can feel yours.

Place your hand upon it now, breathe in:
your breath is the pace of their cooing
your heart is beating with theirs,
the air you breathe inside, their lungs.
Lift up your arms now my sister,
see, you can fly.

Mud Daubers

Mud daubers daubed
the shape of a seed casing
of a poppy head
on the side of the sheet-rocked wall
in my brother's attic,
drawn in by the summer's heat.
What are they doing,
I asked as we ascended
the attic stairs
to view them.
They are crocheting, he answered.
Swallowing my fear
of being stung, I followed,
turned right, and there,
at eye level, sat the symmetrical
nest. *They fly in and out,*
he said, *but they aren't here now,*
hung up on the nests' symmetrical beauty.

Fresh from the Vine

My father stood on his hands to dive off the diving board,
all six foot four inches of him suspended in air,
curling his fingers around the hard edge
of the gritty grey board, and dove off.
He never missed, but one of the last times
I saw him do this, when I was eleven,
his ring cut into his finger from the weight of him.
Down he dove with a sliced finger and his ring
had to be cut off and he needed stitches,
the chlorinated blue pool water acting
as a preliminary antiseptic to clean the wound
as it didn't get infected but I don't remember
if they gave him back two sawn-off halves of the ring,
or if they kept them like they kept the cast
when my cast got sawn off my arm,
broken in two like a loaf of dry French bread
from falling out of the tree house.
I don't know if he got another ring;
I do know his hands held protest signs,
and he freaked me out when he lifted them off
the steering wheel at seventy miles an hour
to light his cigarette, inhaling deeply,
then return one hand on the wheel;
I feared we'd end up off the road.
His hands painted the seventeen steamer trunks
he found to pack with our belongings to move to England.
He adhered striped red and white decals, barbershop style,
onto each trunk and our suitcases to identify them.
I still have one each, with the decals still firmly attached.
I helped him carry these trunks and paint every room
in the houses we moved into.

An industrial engineer, he remains very fond of numbers.
Right now, if you called him, he could tell you exactly
how many tomato plants he has planted: eight,
and how many tomatoes he has picked: seventeen,
and how many on the way: twenty-four.
Legally blind with macular degeneration,
he uses his fingers as his eyes and the shadows
to tell him what to pick: a big red tomato appears
as a brown shadow, as opposed to the nothingness
of the air around it, and that's what he reaches for,
curling his fingers around the shadow
to pick the red ripe tomato that he eats right away.

The Language of Animals

I saw a groundhog today
my father says, a twenty pounder
and stopped his car to watch him.
Another time he saw a hawk.
That was before he was blind
and could no longer drive.
Thirty years earlier,
I smell a turtle, I say,
while riding in the back seat
of the beige station wagon.
My father pulls over, stops the car,
and backs up. *It was here*, I say.
He and I get out and there
is a box turtle smelling of barberry
and humus of moist dried out leaves.
I pick the turtle up
by the diamond edges of its shell.
It sticks its head out
and peers at me, its red eyes
sparkling in the midday sun,
just behind its nose and hard yellow mouth.
A huge passing truck rattles the ground.
The turtle whooshes its head back
into its shell, and closes it,
the arched drawbridge going up.
I place the turtle back down
on its edge of highway
and we return to the car.

Now when my husband comes home,
I ask, *what did you see?* Two hawks,
a deer, some days nothing.
And when we go out, like now,
what will we see, going back an exit,
and pull to the side of the road

to watch two deer. One jerks its head
up straight, startled, sees us watching,
raises its white flag tail, bounds
two leaps away, as its partner inspects us,
blinks its eyes. The other one stamps,
returns three steps, trucks and cars
moving our car in their passing suction of wind.
It's time to go, insists Jim,
unable to bear the traffic whizzing by
any longer. We edge forward;
both deer bound away in beauty;
something I could tell my father,
so he could see again.

Wings
For Debra

And where are you now, my kind friend?
Today is sunshiny and cold, the kind
of day for dragging in wood logs.
Remember when a little brown field mouse
hopped upon your stash of logs inside
your living room, and you, refusing bait,
trapped it with a shoebox,
took your captured friend to a farmer's
field, where he was mowing
the bottom of the field, shearing off corn stalks
in preparation for winter, and you asked
his permission to let your mouse,
sitting up and looking at you in its cage,
go in the field, and he answered yes,
taking you seriously, and how
you made sure to tell me
this story before you forgot you
hadn't told me it, laughter
in your tone, how could the farmer
have said no to you,
a tall winsome white haired
beauty with her age only showing
in her hands as she held up
the box, the mouse, to show him
her treasure, now released,
like you now, released into the
shorn corn fields of heaven,
where everyone has opened up
the doors of the cages and let everyone
and every creature go.

In the Clouds

Seven Canada geese break rank
and glide single file, tiny butlers
of the lake bring me their utter calm,
served on the platter of the lake
I swim upon with them.
Expecting them to scatter, take flight,
they don't, propelled by same
glad joining of feet and body
in water as I am,
three feet away now
gliding through the water
in the same direction.
As rain smatters the surface,
raised nipples upon the water
everyone leaves the beach
except Jim reading a book
huddled under the large oak
holding my sandals,
his shoulders covered with a towel.

Sluice

Challenge greater than rocket ships
traversing sound barriers to Mars
keeping cool in the humid washcloth

of the Virginia weather we're breathing
here on the upper branch of New England
swimming radiant circuits

of arms cutting through green water
cupping back its soft skin over and over
stroke by stroke towards the fronds

that filter oxygen back into the water
on the other side of the lake, the green water
all that is visible, underneath

refrigerated by the earth's cool bosom.
Down below I go to swim with pike
turtles and minnows, holding

my breath long as I can, two lungs
joined as one lung of the lake,
green, there is no bottom,

light filters its careless fingers
caressing my back, then up
to surface water heated by thirsty sun

ceaselessly shining on the water he cannot lift to drink,
so hot even the heron swims, his beak
twisting side to side, alert, so much

of his body under water just like me
only his neck and head suspended in the air

torrential in its humidity
the only air we have to breathe.

The Divinity of Chocolate

I'm doing something bad, she cooed,
pulling a honey coated chocolate bar
from the shelf, and then, another one,

the chocolate the deep dark feathers
of the cliff swallows
she had encouraged to High Ledges

with puddles and white down;
couldn't the milk chocolate be
the scattered pebbles at the puddles' edge?

And the crystallized caramel,
the specks of buff on their underbelly
as the cliff swallow darts in,

sewing the rocks of the cliff together,
and dark chocolate, the curved head
of the barn swallow

she's noticed has vanished,
but she's nourishing them back,
encouraging farmers to keep barn doors open

so the blue of their darting into the night
from dusk remains balm to tired eyes
much as the sweet snap

of the chocolate bars revive cheer,
as she outlines the ledges
where the cliff swallows have returned to nest,

as she draws the lines of the soaring wings
of the barn swallow, chocolate edging the night sky,
their forked tails divining sweet air,

the welcoming of a new home,
the savoring of dark chocolate:
there can be no substitute.

Coda

As I kiss the neck of my beloved
the T-cells in your body are raging.
As I kiss the lids of his eyes,
it is a battle you are waging
stroking his soft side
you recover from surgery
Lip to lip mouth to mouth
you wonder how to cope
Front to front, side to side
you ask to be alone
Neck to neck, palm to palm
I'll have to have chemo
Purging sighing soft
it's a hard row to hoe
Palm to palm, kiss to cheek,
I'm in a lot of pain, you say
Resting heads on pillow
Please call me in a week, you ask
Your T-cells behind my every touch: *I will.*

Clemency

The bobcat that walks firmly across
the snow's crust cares not for the man
or for the red skidder scuttling smoke.
He's watched him leave, he's smelled
the apple core the man threw down, even nibbled
it and spit it out; he tells time by the sound
of his truck leaving, 3 p.m. every afternoon.
And the sounds of the house cause him no alarm.
He's silent and they have not heard him
padding parallel to them on their walk
along the ridge. He cuts across the path
just as they close the door, knowing
precisely how long it will take for them
to get to the path he just crossed
their snuffling boots crunching snow
their silly short dog lunging for sticks.
He gazes with yellow eyes as they walk closer,
ambles away unconcerned.

Treasures of the Earth
For G

How you love words, their shine, their clusters,
their liquid touch, their cayenne pepper bite,
their surprising nectar, a mango easy to cut into,
messy to eat. How you polished them, never hasty,
never overdone, taking your time, pulling the fried
eggs of your poems up, plumping them into toast
just at the right moment, and if the yolk remained
runny you knew how to wipe its too bright yellow away,
to edit its brazen insides if it was showing too much.
But wasn't that what you wanted, the caviar, the tiny
eggs of too much, that cracker thin edge where revealing
became a shawl you could wear, and how you wrote it,
the salt and pepper of words you used, fed you, kept you warm,
that edge, the copper edge of an old dime sharp against
your tongue, where even eating a fried egg sandwich
could be divine when you said who you ate it with,
how you gave the other half to the one you loved.
I give the other half of this sandwich to you.

May the fingers of the nurses who wash you be the words
you loved to polish, to sort through like sea glass and shells.
May the sounds of the nurses' clothes or any machines
be the rustle of the monarch butterflies you let emerge
on the sticks from their cocoon in your neatly kept living room,
their wings as they stretched open and flew; it had a sound
whisper thin but you caught it, loud as an ocean wave crashing
so you could write it down and feed it to us.
May the windows in your room have the blinds pulled wide
so you can see the pearl blue of the open sky
that holds its umbrella open above us at all times,
never closing, its arms never getting tired.

May the sheets that warm your body be light and soft,
may the hands of your husband holding your hand
be the sonnet he may have wished he could write
when writing was your first love, your morning voice.

Released Back into the Wind

In the dusk of winter
a barred owl hurtled
towards the seeds I poured
into the bird feeder, its
destination my eye level
the tray of seeds and morsels it did not
want, only confused by hunger
thought it might. No time to
lift up my arm, I stepped back
and then the owl, a ream of smoke
solidified as himself, brown-eyed,
staring at me from the branch
of the spruce, without a nest,
just the wind to buffet him,
in the trees beside our house.

I left out pieces of bacon; undesired.
I bought him chunks of stew meat,
top quality, though I, a vegetarian,
ate none. He too distained it offered
on a plate. My fingers encased
in thick leather gloves,
I held out the meat in my hand
for him to grasp, and he did, flying
in a rush of tallow-colored wings,
lighting on the phone lines
leading to our house, awake
with all of us when the children
caught the feeder bus.

Sometimes he'd disappear, and at night
when I awoke to a familiar
yet amplified darkness weighing in
and walked to the window
to see if he was perched on the tree,

he was, living inside the dark
beating of my heart as though
whatever longing it was he felt too
or perhaps he was the longing, the wildness
that woke me to keep watch for him.
Some days when he disappeared, I called
owly, owly, and he'd return and I'd lift
my hand. He'd swoop to my feet
to stand and chitter his thanks,
as I lay more meat before him.

But then one evening
as my young daughter clothed in scarf,
coat, and gloves left to feed her
chickens he flew behind her
landing in back of her, the imprint
of his wings like fingers stroked in snow
four feet apart with empty space in between.
Next time he flew to my feet,
I had to stamp them
no, owly, I can't feed you anymore.
He chittered, I stamped my feet,
then he looked up into the wild nest
in my eyes that he had grown to love
and flew away one last time.

Angle

Low into the woods he drives his skidder
the seat patched with silver duct tape,
black grease upon the wheels.
It emits a blue smoke that he
does not worry about, a noise he wears
no shields upon his ears to guard against.
He's been chopping logs for thirty years,
growing apples just the same.
Now they're sending apples from China
packed in Washington, and bought the train station
between the west and east coast,
at prices lower than he can give.
But here the woods, the prices dropped here
too, wood coming in from Russia,
but here the woods, the beeches bend down
to him, their tiny burnt orange cones
sidle along the rust red of his skidder,
and the red lines where the forester left
his painted mark tell him which tree to cut.
And he knows how to hold the chainsaw
hefting its weight in his thighs
holding it like a woman caught in a mid-dip swing
her body cutting into the tree, rhumba, rhumba,
the wedge he must cut first, then on the other side
he slices the saw's teeth through to the heart
when the tree gives way, heaves
with a sigh to the ground, then crashes,
snow fliffing up, leaves and branches scattering.

He knows how to do this, to let them down so easy,
he lets them down all over the woods.
The hard maple bends to him, take me,
she says, take me, I want to rest now
and he holds his saw tight, his thighs perched
and cuts straight into her heart, never missing.

The Other Ninety-Eight Percent

Migrant worker's hands stained green
from picking spinach, green leaves
full of iron he cannot eat, washes
his hands in a bowl in his room
sleeps on a bare mattress on the floor
window glass broken, curtains frayed
their once brilliant yellows whitened
with sun that only tans his face
deeper, squints his eyes when
he walks back out to the rows of spinach
washing his hands in the sprinkler
set for the plants, not allocated
for him, the chuckwagon rolls in, sells
warm bagels and cream cheese, hot coffee
but not Columbian like he drank at home,
the drops of mercy that carried him through
the morning, saving money for his daughter's
communion, the priest's drops of mercy,
holy water touched to her forehead
to protect her, keep her from a future
like this where he bends his back to the hot soil
the green leaves he cannot eat;
they are for sale, not for him.
Maybe at home the corn he planted
has come up, maybe his wife
has already picked the ears, or his son,
what he would give to go back home,
only drops of mercy now
the sweat that rolls down his face
nine o'clock sun and it's already eighty degrees,
and the spinach needs picking before it wilts.

Knowing the Great Unknown

Can I keep an Aborigine
alive in the desert
where he can draw up water
from under the sand
if I recycle my cans
can I keep the leaves green
there in the desert
where even the lizards are parched
if I use less gas, change my oil
can I hold out my hand
across this great distance
if I only use the dryer at night
when electricity use is less
easier to trundle along the wires?
And can I carry you in my arms
through the desert when you have given up
past the kangaroos, errant camels,
if I plant more trees, their leaves
giving oxygen to you, to seep
into the desert air, invisible
but still there for you to breathe?
And if I keep my heat down,
will it bring you more water
underneath the sand where you
dip your straw to sip
while I carry you to my house
so I can lay you down;
I'm carrying you to my house
so I can lay you down.

Invincible

The men were thinking, we'll divert this river
this new river Irene wrought out of roads paved by men
backhoeing chunks of black asphalt with the river's mighty arm
through hayfields, corn fields, pastures with cows about to deliver.

This new river Irene wrought out of roads paved by men
Cold River, Green River, Deerfield River slurried into waves
through hayfields, cornfields, pastures with cows about to deliver
through 8A, Rte. 2, Ashfield Road, banks upheaving rocks;
destructive slaves.

This new river Irene wrought out of roads paved by men
gouging out one ton balustrades, corkscrewing bridge underpinnings
Cold River, Green River, Deerfield River, slurried into waves,
moving houses, mooring barns, propane tanks; Irene's winnings

through hayfields, cornfields, pastures with cows about to deliver
backhoeing chunks of black asphalt with the river's mighty arm
through 8A, Rte. 2, Ashfield Road, banks upheaving rocks;
destructive slaves.
The men were thinking, we'll divert this river.

Basic Training

There was a train but he didn't take it.
Instead he drove his new Civic across
black asphalt, scorched land just after wildfires,
Ohio corn fields, the Mississippi,
Texas panhandle singing to his radio.

Instead he drove his new Civic across
three thousand miles in five days; count 'em,
Ohio corn fields, the Mississippi.
Reaching each motel, he jogged, keeping fit.

Texas panhandle singing to his radio,
he saw no animals, just one large hawk.
Instead he drove his new Civic across
desert, Oklahoma, New Mexico.

Three thousand miles in five days; count 'em.
Black asphalt scorched land just after wildfires,
Ohio corn fields, the Mississippi.
There was a train but he didn't take it.

Early Thanksgiving Migration

On our way back home on the train
from your basic training graduation,
we watch the dried grass, mesquite,
pinon, and terra cotta adobe homes high
in the Sandia Mountains.
In the San Felipe Pueblo
a pink hog, gutted, lies
on its side, its squat people
surrounding it eye the passing train,
the round prickly pears stubby and burned
black by the sun, arroyos dry,
footprints fleshed out in its red sand,
dirt-bike tracks fresh.
As we speak your name
a gathering of cranes flash
before the window, stalking green fields
irrigated underground, their intermittent
bending for barley, final harvest,
cranes such as you had seen
driving the back roads in Artesia
flush with dried out sparse green leaves
and the hard green fists of pecans in orchards
waiting for our train to come in,
cranes tall as emus gliding, you said
and here the cranes,
the only time we see them,
as we lift your name to the wind.

Barren

Barren barns scattered amongst short corn field
not a year for high yield, drought shrinking peeled
kernels, cost of irrigation, vernal
dream still farmer's hope, his own eternal
wish that water would seep from holes dug deep
maybe dug by elves while he's lost to sleep
irrigation too costly, banks too strict
buried saints in yards, tried every trick
to get water to fall not thrown by storms,
battling thirsty plants, against nasty worms
vulnerable kernels, early stage corn
farmer's wife bows her head, praying first son
of God will station clouds above their house
starving for water for fields, washing blouse.

Desert Sand

In the kitchen I invoke your name
praying to the angels
and infant Saint of Atocha
patron saint of weary travelers
green to hold you whole
to have your house offer accepted,
the broken pieces of candles
you found in the desert,
a lost shrine to the saint
discovered beneath layers of sand
flung by winds, clang of metal
candle holders, their glass no longer whole,
only you alone, a stream before you opening
though there is no water, and stuck in the sun
as even the lizards were, but
the diamondback rattlers now are hiding,
you wanted no home for them, only for yourself,
one you had worked so hard to get.

Right of First Refusal

Don't pray for me anymore
say the grey whales
birthing calves
off the Pacific coast.

Don't pray for me anymore
say the right whales
siphoning plankton and krill
off the Atlantic coast.

Don't pray for me
squawk the seagulls
pedaling pizza
on the beach in Ocean Park,
their beaks full of crust.

Don't pray for me
says my father,
I don't want anything.

Don't pray for me
mews the tiny black and white
kitten under the stairwell
at the Econo Lodge in Columbus,

it is not your pieces of chicken
that saved me, nor your water
though I was dying of thirst.
I can make it on my own.

Hospice Nurse Drives Home

Not believing anymore in surprises,
late at night, Nurse Jean's car
spins out on sludge rain
a spot hidden from the sun
that never dries out,
the moisture of the Yuba River below
splashing up invisibly 300 feet
to the asphalt above it,
a coat of water
that your tires tried to drink
spinning 180 degrees
and then your car rolls two times
over, count 'em, glass breaking,
sage crumbling, papers flying
and there you land flump, upside down
caught by trees you love so much you've learned
their names, *madrone oaks*,
stopping your descent, holding your car up,
spotted by flashlights held by a dark-haired boy,
Dallas, and his two friends who hold their bodies
against you for warmth in the cold night air
after he pulls you out.
No, you protest, but there,
he pulls, and you finally
hit the ground the car was trying
so hard to meet, the car crumpled
like a candy wrapper, your journals,
nursing papers scattered, and here you wait

for the rescuers to strap
you onto the stoke's sled
and up you come, like an angel
still here on earth,
my intrepid friend,
handed your life back
as a bowl of sweetmeats to savor,
as though a second birth.

Commissioned

I ask myself how is it
I am walking on this snow crusted
path thinking not of my son

but of the birch trees' pink inner bark
and how my dog has learned to wait,
how I have left the knapsack of worry

about the danger my son works in,
I have left it somewhere on a rock
in the woods, somehow I have dropped

it without seeing where it landed.
I will leave it there,
wish him only happiness;

I have left knapsacks all over
the forest, so many I could trip on them
but the coyotes must have carried

them back to their dens for me,
torn them open, set the worry free,
kept the tattered cloth

as a bed for their kits
just born this morning.

Thanksgiving

Thanks for the elephants that don't forget,
how they lumber miles to visit each other,
their own Thanksgiving, squirting
each other's backs with water, trumpeting
their arrival, flapping their ears
to hear better and keep the flies away.
Can they hear us now scribbling
with our pens; do they wish we would
write a poem with one of them in it?
Here Senior Elephant,
place your platter-size foot upon the page
your pebble toes again the gold leaf
edging the china,
I will speak for you:
desert sun and desert moon
desert sand and desert grass
how your feet can feel the tremble
of underground water, an oasis
in the distance that is real,
and there you tumble
in the murky brine,
no alligator or crocodile
your enemy.
Ah, the relief of water over your eyes,
its caress over your back,
how it holds all of you
and gives nothing away.

California's Rose

Ponderosa, too proud to beg,
will not beg for water;
instead she thickens her trunk,
reaches deeper with her roots,
drenching for water underground
without a holding tank
to maintain it, the phloem
between bark and her heart,
the motivation for living,
how she stands with others
bracing the forest, holding
the mountain ledge in place.

Ponderosa, a tree of dreaming,
though forest fires stream
around, and through her,
sometimes surviving with charred bark,
sometimes not, the intense heat
accelerating her growth, decades
of timed growing whittled to minutes;
if her heart can sustain it,
she'll outlive the fire;
if her heart cracks,
she'll be fodder for its burning.

Beards of Moss

The beards of moss on the redwoods in John Muir's woods
catch the high wind, the clamor of squirrels, the gaze
of passersby, just as they did when John Muir first saw them,
and knew they must be preserved,
seeking as he was for perfect forests and found Muir Woods,
the green beards thick yet flush against the trunk
much as his own long beard sat flush upon his neck,
protecting him from cold and vigorous winds,
and the heat of summer or windburn from too long
stuck on glacial outcroppings, which he loved
the best, always seeking more, defying wind
and defying death, defying nature's tyranny,
and the cracks of fissures that could widen at will.
An aloof little dog named Stickeen followed him on one
of his treks, only balking when asked to cross a final ice bridge
the only way they could get back to camp.
Not used to begging, Muir badgered, demanded,
but still Stickeen declined crossing,
as he understood the depth of the crevasse below.
Finally Muir bent on his hands and knees,
reaching for the dog, then made as if to leave him.
Stickeen crossed it, shuddering,
holding his tiny body flat against the ice bridge
crossing death to the other side,
and crawled up the glacier's ice lip
to drink the air and caper, ki-yi-yipping
and follow Muir back to camp
only his aloofness broken, no bones.
Waiters hid under tables, behind curtains
to hear Muir tell the tale of Stickeen,
and even now the moss beards rustle his name.

Taking Off

All the way from the Bridge of the Gods
Nurse Jean pressed Pearl's gas pedal down,
go, go, I want to see that first snow,
though it was ninety-five degrees
with no air conditioning,
the promise of being planted
inside her new home firmly by Christmas
wearing a navy Peacoat and insulated boots
standing out in the white snow
kept her going, kept her cool
as perspiration soaked her back, her thighs,
as daylight expanded and trucks
rocked Pearl as they passed,
caught her up in their wake,
on tidal waves of speed, eighty-five miles
an hour, and she couldn't get off,
the smell of cow dung and refried beans
hanging in the air, cornfield after cornfield.
This is America, she told herself,
as two church congregations prayed for her,
as she, the lone woman,
gunned for Massachusetts,
her heart a spring that wouldn't
let her rest until today,
when the first snow fell
and she could taste it, cold, on her tongue.

The Distance

To travel on your tongue
cross hot sand, tidal pools,

is that not the work of snails,
periwinkles, conchs and whelks,

constantly lifting the edge
of your tongue, your feet,

the snail climbing over crystalized dirt,
up the tomato plant's leaf,

or leaf of an eggplant and devouring it.
The taste of the earth your entrée, your dessert,

the sharp lemon tang of tomato leaves your perfume.
Does the earth tell you her secrets as you linger?

Does she exhale the heaviness of oil and radiant heat?
So brave you are to trundle across stones, or sand

while I sleep, so secure, for there's
nothing else you must do.

Land of the Living

It is late April and night peepers sleep;
it is too warm right now for them to weep.

They want a cool night, to turn on spring's lathe,
awaking in the pond where wood ducks bathe.

Too warm for them and too cold for my Dad
resting in his pond of electric bed, glad

to close his eyes and breathe, oxygen on,
waiting for Rachel Maddow, nighttime fawn

who only speaks through airways, her hollow
full of lights, as though the sun she swallows;

as soon as the lights are dim, she retreats
back into the deep woods on sneakered feet,

a fawn who speaks English, siphons the news,
that now is keeping my Dad living, glued.

Return of the Tigers

Steadily placing padded paw on parched plateau,
stripes hiding his hauteur, his intent,
shadows of banyan trees shield his black stripes,
as he steps into the clearing to taste the dusty sky
nilgais raced through quarter hour ago;
tiger inhales the estrogen levels of their stress,
the cortisol and protein released in molecules of their breath.
He strides, stretching out his length as though yawning
while the nilgais stampede, tiring out.
One falls, which is what he wanted,
though fully capable of leaping and breaking necks.

The land gives him everything he needs:
he barely has to want it
and the nilgais and wild boars appear.
He barely has to feel rumbling in his long belly
to note rumbling of their past stampede,
the width of his paws feeling their tremble,
how they shook the ground.

It is all so easy,
living on the edge, as he does,
the edge of hunger with no refrigerator.
If it rains, he crouches under banana grove leaves,
and licks his paws to quench his thirst.

If he is lonely, he stretches open his wide mouth
and roars.
God hears.

Saving the World

Who am I to deny
that patting my dog, Tyndall,
might be, is, saving the world
that the blast, the sonic boom
of her happiness, the swish of her tail
when I say, *treat*,
her willing open mouth
swallowing such gratitude,
crunching it, demolishing it
and asking for more without shame,
begging, in fact, without remorse,
who is to say that the ripples
from the repeated concentric circles
of her tail wagging, *yes, yes, yes*,
the whole end of her body circling
yes, yes, yes, that these circles
do not vibrate, sonic boom
their happiness to nuns praying
for lost souls, for renters
down to their last dime,
for those riding the bus
on their long commute,
easing their hearts.

Cormorants

Crowded cormorants clutch the clusters of barnacle covered rocks
beside the bore, the surging current of Scornton Creek
scorching towards open sea, side-winding by sandbar of rocks.

Jim carefully courses the egg-sized stones on the concave side
teetering in flip-flops to cushion sharp edges
leaps into the surging tide coursing by the cormorants

clustered on barnacled-covered boulders, Atlantis
emerging as the tide wears down. He careens to the mouth
at the sandbar bend, water level drops two feet, dumps him

after fighting against the tide corralled by glassy stones,
scorched by sand, emerges like the first born man
from the surf to leap into the bore again.

Blinded by the Sun

The tide rising each morning
at a different time, a different height,
a different length, tied to the moon
as it is, rising with prediction
so men set their watches by it,
wait for low tide for the golden sand bars
to emerge, walk out into the water
to dip their arms for sand dollars.
How even the lone seal has set
his watch by the tides' rising,
coming to greet the man and woman
their legs thigh high in sea water
as they walk the sand bar's length.
He has watched them for days now,
and come close, eight feet away,
the day he broke his fast
of solitude, having lived
three years now alone at Scornton Creek
and he is so tired of fish,
they all swim away in fear
but not these two,
they stand still, staring back
into his face, one they cannot see
exactly, blinded by the sun,
just the shape of it
stuck above pale blue water,
they do not look away,
then he dips down,
broken by their acceptance.

Moving Further up the Coast

Clear balloon like creature, submarine shaped
with small yellow orange and pink dots draped

along its body, tiny beads for eyes
and tendrils on its bottom, a surprise

swishing through the salt sea water, small as
my hand disappearing into morass

of bright green sea lettuce waving on rocks
but tide is leaving and this creature balks

from swimming with current into the sea
squishes against rocks covered with wavy

green troll hair, but he'll dry up in the sun
and die if he doesn't hurry up and run

into tidal sluice, so I herd him out,
guide him with my hand towards ocean, turned about,

this squid moving up the coast, weather's burst,
hotter, never seen one before, my first.

First Swim

Ettalynn toddles out into the warm water of the lake
as though it were only air up to her shoulders,
then her mom pulls her forward so she can kick
her legs, dipping her face like a teeter totter doll
into the water for a taste, then fast up,
smiling, her one long bottom tooth
the only pearls she wears.

Crossing the Great Divide

Wondering if my mother
can see the orange orchids
of the touch-me-knots,
so tall they reach my head,
their green beads I press,
spirals of seed leaping out,
if she sees my horse Cinnamon
calmly chewing her hay
divining the ground
for each perfect mouthful,
if she feels the languid waves
caress my shoulders as I breaststroke
across the lake to where the lily pads grow
and back again, if she feels
the sun hot upon my shoulders;
she would have used coconut oil,
Coppertone, her breath
smelling of Pall Malls.
Does she taste the ripe blackberry
that nature has given free,
its tart sweetness,
or nubbin of raspberry?
Or hold her great-grandchildren
as I hold them in my lap
in the water, as the pike
and bass nibble our toes
as I walk offering her my eyes
to see with, my mouth for tasting,
my arms for embracing;
the door is always open.

About the Author

Laura Rodley is a Pushcart Prize winner, quintuple Pushcart Prize nominee, and quintuple Best of Net nominee, with work in *Best Indie Lit NE*. Publisher Finishing Line Press nominated her *Your Left Front Wheel Is Coming Loose* for a PEN L.L. Winship Award and Mass Book Award. FLP also nominated her *Rappelling Blue Light* for a Mass Book Award. Former co-curator of the Collected Poets Series, Rodley teaches the As You Write It memoir class and has edited and published *As You Write It, A Franklin County Anthology Volumes I-VI*, also nominated for a Mass Book Award. She was accepted at Martha's Vineyard's NOEPC and has been a consecutive participant in the 30 poems in 30 days fundraiser for the Literacy Project. Her book *Counter Point* was published by Prolific Press.

www.ingramcontent.com/pod-product-compliance
Lightning Source LLC
LaVergne TN
LVHW041306080426
835510LV00009B/876